A Simple Message to brighten your day

I'm thinking about I care about what happens to You. I want to share your sorrow, and sing your joys.
I am here to talk whenever you need me, always remember how important you are to me.
Know that you are loved. Have a bright beaming better than average day for me.
I dedicated this Book to the ones who have inspired me to write the poems I have and showed me different sides of life.
I especially want to thank my husband Robert and Our Children Jessica, Caleb and Megan for supporting me with their Love and devotion of all my writing.

## What You've Given Me

To give back what you've given to me, would take me nearly and eternity.

Through all the special times we've shared, you've helped me to learn, love, and care.

All the hard times we've last through.

Help to show our love is true.

To give back to you, what you've given me, would take nearly eternity, but if that what it takes, it what I'll do to show the love I feel for you.

## Eternity

I look into your eyes and all that I see us the burning desire you have for me.

No words need to be spoken, no feelings need to be shared.

Everyone can feel it, it's in the air.

Our love is undying it will never go away.

We'll still be together when we're old and gray, even after all we've been through I will always and forever love you.

## Your Touch

You touch my hands and the coolness, shivers through my body.

You touch my arms and the warmth passes through my heart.

You touch my face ad the caring travels through my mind.

You touch my lips and the passion burns through my soul.

You touch me and I know what it is to feel alive.

## Love

Just saying that I Love You doesn't mean a thing at all.

For Loving words fly like the birds, when they hear the winters call.

Love is a thing that proves itself a thousand times a day.

In the simple little things you do, and the little things you say.

Love is a thing called sacrifice, a tonic when your blue.

Love is the joy of doing things for someone dear to you.

## True Friend

True Friend will always defend you.

True Friend will never pretend.

True Friend is there to lend a ear, shoulder to help mend.

True Friend is there to spend time with you without end.

True Friend is lie Heaven Amen.

## Key To My Heart

I had closed the door upon my heart and wouldn't let anyone in.

I had trusted and loved only to be hurt.

But that would never happen again, I had locked the door and tossed the key as hard and as far I could.

Love would never enter there again.

My heart was closed for good, then you came into my life and make me change my mind.

Just when I thought that tiny key was important to find, that when you held out your hand and proved to me I was wrong, Inside your palm was the key to my heart you had it all along.

## Hearts Sadness

Hearts sadness us like no other madness.

Hearts sadness is like a depression that leaves an impression.

Hearts sadness is a misery that brings out misty tears.

Hearts sadness is you must be apart at times.

Hearts sadness can hit you like a dart.

Hearts sadness can be the start of a new Heart of Happiness.

## Blooming Rose Of My Heart

I'm laying here late at night thinking of your silky touch, against mine in moonlit night. Two bodies intertwined in the deep heart of summers light.

Your smile is sweet as wine that brings out mine. Your sweet wine like smile I hold in my heart as if we never part cause we will always be in each other hearts.

I knew from the start you would be a part of my heart, like a Blooming Rose Bud fresh smelling and new, so I could never be blue cause I have you.

You have such a magnetic excitement which desires a devoted attachment of pleasurable enlightenment that makes me want to ignite your passionate fires.

Slowly, Gently, touching, busting over your body way into the night, letting you know everything is alright, as your heart takes flight into my arms.

## Love Always

Love when days are glad and golden.

Love when sorrows make thy days gray.

Love when health is ever splendid.

Love if should go away comes back.

Love when friends are fine and loyal.

Love if any prove untrue, whatsoever life may bring you.

Love is always for you.

## Truth And Love

The things we do will soon be past unless we do the things that last.

The life we build may never stand for sinking sand.

The wordy thing for which we slave can never bring us from the grave.

The things above like truth and love will always be eternity.

## Hurt Feelings

When you hurting inside and feel like huge tide coming over you head.

When you keep your chin up high you will win.

When things start to subside a grin will begin.

When the feelings go through your skin, and you have cried so much that your head spins, go within wide eyed and know it okay not to hide your feelings inside.

When you tried and not lied you will have pride in yourself and to think it all begin with a grin.

## True As The World Is Round

My love for you is as true as the world is round.

I twirled through the world to pursue a view, a clue, of my love for you.

I found my love for you could at times be surrounded with the blues.

I threw you a clue to make our love a new.

I found my love for you pound through my heart when I found you to untrue, I fell to ground.

I swirled around in my head as it started to brew, and I found myself come unglued.

I have a wound in my heart that will hound me with no sound.

I found one thing will never be untrue, that is my love for you as true as the world is round.

## Best Friend

Best Friend so far away, knows how to make my day feel like Heaven rays.

Best Friend so away know how I feel and I never have to say a single word.

Best Friend so far away is nothing but blur in the life here on earth.

Best Friend so far away is really in Heavens rays cause no one truly knows me here and not seem to care to know the breathe of me only Our Lord truly knows me.

Best Friend so far away is really Heavens rays cause Our Lord is My Best Friend in Heavens Rays that shines on earth today.

## Inner Feelings

An inner feeling of things to happen before they do that you can not choose.

When it happens you seems to lose, no matter hat you say or do, it leaves you feeling

worthless and whose feelings are for you to say and do, are not always what we choose.

 Find yourself feeling the blues, remember feelings are those we can not always

choose sometimes feelings are to lose a part of you and become a different, better you.

Special Teacher

A special teacher fulfills me in my heart, that builds skills in me.

A special teacher sunny smiles flies over hills that warms in miles of style.

A special teacher beautiful inside and out.

A special teacher guides and gives me prides inside wide eyed that will mot subside.

A special teacher that provides me with skills, that will reside and can not be denied as I slide in life worldwide.

## Springtime

It is a time of trees blooming with leaves, I watching them blow in the wind.

All the beauty blooms before our eyes as each surprises of a new day born.

It is a certain excitement to see flowers bloom and yards being inviting by the delight of their sightless.

A storm in springtime can warm or come and scorn like a thorn and warn.

It brings the winds lightening and thunder, and kind of the storm to cling and zing and swing as it fingers on.

As it calms the air is fresh and new, sky is blue, through the clouds news a view of a rainbow who would know Spring sprang through a chain that will always remain true.

## Kindred Souls

I feel comfortable with you, as you do with me, and we understand like kindred souls.

We meet again and already know each other and touched leased from another lifetime ago.

I've known you for years in my soul, and my soul cheers with tears as my soul is yours it appears.

I feel it when you laugh, when you sad, when your angry, that half of your soul becomes whole as if I stole it as my goal.

I am glad to know you are the one who is my kindred soul.

I am not sure if anyone knows how we can see by looking in each other eyes and our souls rise to the sky.

We know kindred souls like ours will never say bye, we will always live high in the sky that never tell a lie.

## My Dad

My Dad never said out loud "I Love You" to me, but will always know he does.

My Dad never had love of parents to show what love was.

My Dad never let me go without things I needed.

My Dad told me once he not know how to love but I tell you, he does indeed know.

He was always there growing up for me, whatever I needed help with.

My Dad and I do not always agree except for he wanted me to succeed, and not be taken over by greed.

My Dad however he grew up knows hows to love me, by talking to me, even though he not always understand me way I am.

My Dad can tell me he never will know how to love but I will know forever in my heart, he does know how to love.

My Dad and I are alike in so many ways, so in my heart I know he loves me as a Dad should his daughter who so much like he.

I Love You Dad You Always Be With Me In My Heart And Every Part Of Me.

## My Husband

You were there for me in High School where we met. In good times and bad just as today.

You swept me off my feet like a jet taking off to the skies.

You and I did not let anyone keep us from ties we shared inside our hearts.

You were my Sweetheart then as you are today.

I know no matter what lies are told what we hold in our hearts, we will never part.

You are my Sweetheart and will forever be in my heart.

## Hard Times

It hard to see those we care about and love us in all situations as they may be leave us.

It to understand what God reason is for situation of life.

It hard at times to keep our head high.

It hard to see from our eyes of tears why God makes us cry.

It hard to pray with so much pain, but we must look beyond the rain of tears and pain, and see what all we have to gain and remember to pray everyday.

It hard to know what the rays of Heaven will be like so we have to pray so our life on earth rays.

## Life Journey

Life can make you sad and confuse you.

Life can make you glad and smile.

Life can point us to God as we follow him, accept His Love in our hearts.

Life is full of disappointments we not expect.

Life is non-ending miles as God leads us to become stronger.

Life is to prepare us; Gods Child to learn, to love us He loves us, for one day we will join Him in Heaven above we will know only then how much love He has for us, so we trust in Him.

## Thorn Of Roses

Life is not always a bed of petals of roses. It has thorns to go with it too.

Life is like a Rose, beautiful, sweet smelling, and nice to look at.

Life is like a Rose sometimes thorns hurts and makes you bleed

with sadness.

Life is like a Rose beautiful, pleasant to look at, delicate, full of many colors

to see and makes you smile.

Life is like a thorn of a Rose sometimes makes you hurt in many ways, being

cautious of what may come your way.

Life of Roses must have thorns to make the Rose more beautiful when

it comes your way.

## Growing Girls

As Girls and become teenagers they bossy and emotional.

As girls grow and become teenagers mommy becomes more noisy and and filled with more feelings of emotions.

As girls grow and become teenagers mommy is lousy at making them feel better they know it all they seem to think.

As girls grow and teenagers they lie, and take things and think mommy in a daze all day, and not know.

As girls grow and become teenagers and have tantrums, mommy becomes like phantom of the Opera.

As girls grow and become teenagers mommy treasures the pleasures of being alone at home, or roam to the store for talk on phone, or just being down right bored.

## Follower Of God

God answers our prayers just take time sometimes we have to wait in line.

We continue to pray and follow our relationship with God we know in mind, all good takes time.

He always hears us, and has time for us, since God knows no time as we do.

When our prayers are answered it not as we always expect or where we are looking.

Hooking us to follow a path only God knows best for so we can have a bit of rest as we continue our quest to follow God.

Answers to our prayers gets us to see things that brings tears of joy that we once feared.

Praying allows us to bond with those we love, and above all, be follower of God for all time.

Jessia

Girl so strong who has coming along way, I must say.

As I pray for her as she recovers spirits stay high, trying all she has to do to recover.

It hard to watch as she does suffer with pain through out body using her muscles that have tightened.

Girl so strong as days move along she enlightens day with the brightness of her beauty.

As mommy helps her more she sees a new side that tightens their bond like beauty of a song.

Girl so strong, knows for sure now that mommy love is like no other in the world.

## God's Hospitality Of Interfaith

There are certain ones in life that you meet; and greet you with caring arms, when life seems to be tearing you up inside.

There are ones that part of Interfaith Hospitality Network so caring, and loving, giving their support through Interfaith to let you know God is still watching over you, when things seem impossible.

This is a network that makes you work through hands of God in ways to help you follow God in hospitality of all His houses uniting you as His Children.

There are things all possible through following God of Interfaith the Hospitality of people Networking making you inside a follower of God sharing His love making all things possible again.

Letter To Her Solider

Miles apart and you're off to war.

Without you here, its hard to tell if its night or day anymore.

I think deep thoughts of lips and touch and wonder if I will ever feel you again.

My heartaches and craves for your warmth late at night in this big empty bed.

Every evening I watch the news and hold our children close to me while they sleep.

I pray for your safe return to us.

Please be brave out there and know you are not alone.

In faith and in my heart, I know we will be together soon forever,

Forever Yours<br>Your Ever<br>Loving'<br>Wife

## Unhappiness I Feel

Unhappiness is something I feel all the time.

Unhappiness is something I feel inside, and cry all the time.

Unhappiness is something I feel but I can hide.

Unhappiness is something I feel because I have no idea what like to have a child.

Unhappiness is something I feel when all friends around me know like to have a child of own from birth.

Unhappiness is something I feel of a worthlessness.

Unhappiness is something I feel and wonder why I was put on earth when all it seems I end up getting hurt.

Unhappiness is something I feel when I think I do right things and all I get back is negative attitude.

Unhappiness is something is something I feel and know I always I will. There is no true happiness for me on earth.

Unhappiness is something I feel when I have to give into things to make someone else happy.

Unhappiness is something I feel when I pretend like all okay.

Unhappiness is something I feel I always will feel.

## Thoughts Of You

Thoughts of you make my heart flutter and sing.

Thoughts of you makes me dream of my commitment to you totally from my heart.

Thoughts of you makes me want to utter to the world my love for you.

Thoughts of you makes me want to think of the rings we will give each other to show our love will not break apart.

Thoughts of you makes me know that everything will forever be alright as long as I have you as my beloved.

## Make Wishes

Wishes are only that, Wishes.

Wishes are what you want or need but can not always come true.

Wishes are only in our dreams when we sleep.

Wishes are only what we have to try to change things we not like.

Wishes are only to help us feel some security with hope to change what makes us sad for hopes to be glad.

## Look In Mirror

Look around Look in mirror what do I see when I look at me?

Look around, Look in mirror what do I see I want to be?

Look around, Look in mirror what do I see that I once dreamed to be?

Look around, Look in mirror what do I see that I never want to be?

Look around, Look in mirror what do I see that is so good about me?

Look around, Look in mirror what do I see that will live in others when when I no longer will be?

Look around, Look in mirror what I see is a girl, who now a woman, who gave sweetness to all she knew who is now a woman who had so many dreams of what her life would be, and only failed at all she did and does.

Look around, Look in mirror what I see is a woman who is caught up in making others happy, and never has time to make her mark in the world and does what she not see for her in the broken mirror.

## All She Can Do

She can do all she can for someone to please him and he still complains,

that makes her feel like she going insane.

To keep herself from being insane she has to just find something to escape it all.

It has to always be about how all involved feels since it not at all the same.

She gets to the point that she feel stuck in the middle being pushed at both

sides, and just not strong enough to hold herself up no more, only torn like a tissue.

Everything seems to become a issue and all she want to is make the peace.

There is never an end to the words that are said to her that always made to

feel guilty or ashamed of wanting to be happy.

She has been pushed from one side so long that it seems easier to be stronger

a little more there since knowing that side pushing has grown weak, and not really able to know

how to pull her closer to him anymore.

She knows that she has to be stronger and deal with him that hurts her in

every-way and stay so can see her children everyday, since he has told her never see them

again and so that would be the end of any in her.

## My Love For You

My Love for you, will last it is strong, and I know we belong like a song,

so it can not be wrong, for you crossed my path, I am so thrilled, for you fulfill me in a way

that means a lot and hits all the right spots.

My Love for you will last, I will forget you not, you have my heart in a

windsor knot that has caught it, now a true lovers knot, to never be untied cause there is no

reason for lies for us two, who are close to falling In Love as I seem to be in my first sight view.

## First Glance

At first glance I knew you were well worth the chance I took.

At first glance I knew you put my heart in a trance.

At first glance my heart began to dance.

At first glance my heart sparked like a song that enhanced to dance.

At first glance you cast a gaze in my eyes that showed no lies only to

ties that would rise to last through the years forever my dear.

Desire So Strong

You are like the song I love to sing, to which everyday seems like spring.

As I went through each day to find a way to belong in this world before you came along it all just seemed wrong, and I felt a strong desire still and continued the will to try to zoom along, but the thrill of it all just was gone to fill my heart to feel that I belonged to one I have feelings for so strongly, like the blinding sun will never be done shining.

  I have now won a place in the world as I know I am yours and we are bound together like we share organs inside you and I

## My Tears

Sometimes I just cannot bear no more I swear.

I feel myself stare and totally unaware of the tears on their way.

I usually have a flair to share a deep brightness to make things into

fight, I not able to make alright.

Just not have strength in me to deal with all this despair and I feel so scared.

## Closed Off My Heart

I closed off my heart, to keep it from those who causes it pain and keep me from going insane.

I closed off my heart, so my brain can stay clear, and steer where it should be.

I closed off my heart, it just seems to me those in my life are not as they appear to others.

I closed off my heart trying to be smart to keep the part of my heart that works the art.

I closed off my heart, to try to figure out what really in my heart that has been broken in so many ways.

I closed off my heart, for there are things I know even though I am not told, just blown off and told No to all that I know I know, and sure can prove.

I closed off my heart, so that I can remove all the love I use to have for all of you.

I closed off my heart, to remove all the damage that still could be done from all of you who choose to lie to me.

I closed off my heart, that now there is no longer a part that will grow for those who brought me woe.

I closed off my heart, now to all those who you will never be able to know.

## Should I Stay Or Go

I keep going over it in my head, if I should stay or go.

I keep the one reason to stay, close to my heart, as I ask should I stay or go.

I keep saying don't let the reason to stay open more more of my heart as I ask should I stay or go.

I keep going through each day for the reason, the one who needs me to stay, yet I ask should I stay or go.

I keep asking should I stay or go and I know only one reason makes me stay and go, do you know?

What has made me stay still today and go?

## If You Care To Listen

Listen to my plea, or I may flea, and not continue to be where you can see me.

If you care to listen I can share with you the key you once held in heart so I not flee thee.

If you care to listen, then don't talk to me as if I am dumb, so I become gleam and feel numb.

If you care to listen, just beware, because my heart can not bare no more despair, I swear.

If you care to listen you may find something rare in my words I pray to want to stay.

If you care to listen, then don't snap at me, it weighs on our marriage and pushes me away.

If you care to listen, you need to find a way to make it worth my while to stay

Love just isn't enough anymore to keep us from decay.

## Tears In My Eyes

If you were a tear in my eyes, I would never cry.

If you were a tear in my eyes, I would wipe you away.

If you were a tear in my eyes, I would cherish your drops.

If you were a tear in my eyes, I would love your tears as my own.

If you were a tear in my eyes, I would see the color like rain drops after when it rains.

If you were a tear in my eyes, its the fear of losing and a broken heart that says it the end.

## Heart And Soul

I'm your heart and soul, but a tear would not be alone.

I'm your heart and soul, but a tear I would not wipe away from your face.

I'm your heart and soul, but a tear would not lose the true love and compassion
I have for you.

I'm your heart and soul, but a tear would see the color like a rainbow
through my eyes.

I'm your heart and soul, but a tear of tears of joy stream down my face, arms
wide open of love for you.

I'm your heart and soul, but a tear from God gave me you again.

I'm your heart and soul, but a tear as God say as I care, you throw your
throw your time of hurt.

I'm your heart and soul, but a tear shine knowing my love for you will shine
throughout the trails of life, as we are made one.

Sisters To Us From God

Sisters who are sent to us from God, are angels in disguise, that become our friends as well.

Sisters who are sent to us from God, come from all over the world to chat with online and everywhere we may meet them.

Sisters who are sent to us from God, are to help us through the tough times, to confide in.

Sisters who are sent to us from God, know how to make us smile and laugh and forget all the hurts.

Sisters who are sent to us from God, know our heart and feel our pain and joys.

Sisters who are sent to us from God, give us back ourselves that we lost for

awhile cause we forgot to smile due to all the fails of our life.

## Thinking Of You

My Darling, I think of you while I am awake, I think of you while I am asleep.

My Darling, as I think of you holding me in your arms as we hold each other.

My Darling, I think of you every time I blink my eyes.

My Darling, I think I am on the brink of falling In love with you.

My Darling, I think of you, and know I do not want to let go of you, I want only to take hold of you for rest of my life, I feel blessed to have you.

My Darling, I think of you, and in my heart I know I would love to be your wife, it just that I can not depart from the woe of my life I chose, and must not I know stray.

My Darling, I think of you and know I will never betray you in heart you have it all I can give, it will only grow stronger day after day.

My Darling, I think of you and know my feelings for you could get carried away, and may let my passion play as you show me the way and I will never let you break away from, and get you to stay and we can forever be together whenever where ever day after day.

## Princess

A princess is not all the royalty, she all about beauty poise.

A Princess beauty is one who glows with lot of love to give.

A Princess who glows with love in her heart us happy with life.

A Princess can light up a room with her smile.

A Princess is spoiled and loved by the one who has the key to her heart.

A Princess is one who always wants to make the one love of hers happy and always smile.

## My Love

My love for you came unexpectedly.

My love for you I am not ashamed.

My love for you will not stay the same.

My love for you grows just as we do with age.

My love for you has me in a daze.

My love for you will last all days of my life.

## They Do Not Know Me

There are things some do not know about me, only they would take time.

I can be hard to get to know or easy to know, if only they cared enough to look at me.

My eyes are my feelings of the inner me, all they need to do is, to see me through

my eyes, that change colors just like a mood ring with lot of blue.

I am open, honest, and in in lot of pain all over one inside, and out, if only they

take the time to know me and would see the true me.

## The Way I Feel In Your Arms

Your hands so strong and gentle I yearn and love to trust them.

I have your arms around me, holding me tightly as I learn to turn you on.

Your kisses so loving and passionate.

Your body next to mine touching so warm wanting to be closer.

Inside you make me burn with passion and all I want is to be in arms as we earn each other trust and lust until dusk.

## Survive

Sometimes we meet people that bring so much to our lives, at times when we think we not survive.

Find that we have so much in common that drives us closer together and the lives we have, we know will strive.

As we dive into getting to know each other gives us a new understanding that forgives

and lets us live to arrive to each day with high fives cause we have a reason to survive.

## No One Seem To Notice

I am here, but sometimes no one seems to notice.

I am talking, but sometimes no one seems to notice.

I am here, not talking sometimes no one seems to notice, I just to scream.

I am here, but feel like I not have any steam.

I am talking, but sometimes feel I in a dream in extreme loneliness not really on anyone team.

## God Is Around Is

God is around us, we open our eyes we will see.

God is around for us to talk to, and show we believe in Him.

God is around for us even though He makes no sound, He has ways to show us He cares.

God around for us, we come as we are to His house for He sees us everyday, and loves us.

God is around for us, as we pray, play, cry, and having a bad day.

God is around for us, all we need to do is follow Him and pray, He will show us the way.

## Thin Line Between The Head And Heart

We always were told to put our head and heart together, and not whine to be lead to the sign from our heart and shine.

We are blind by those being kind to play with our mind.

We whine to find what we been fed all our lives, through the vine to find our head and heart doesn't make us smart.

There is a thin line between the head and heart that makes us dart from the art of a heart that is kind.

We wed to find a thin line between the head and the heart.

# Home

Home is a place where love begins with grins.

Home is a place where mom embraces love that could never be erased.

Home is a place where somethings are to be discreet.

Home is a place worth the sweet grace of growing space.

Home is a place where love is concrete like on a street.

Home is a place where you should not cheat, it not a race that can be beat.

Home is a place where feet brace on a concrete place that should greet with sweet calm embrace which shows on our face.

Sadness

Sadness is a feeling that fills our hearts, like no other feeling, it takes away a large part of our heart we need for love to care for those we become close to.

It rips and tears through all our feelings and we not feel very smart.

Hanging onto life with a feeling in our heart like a knife cutting you all out until you can not feel the sharpness no more, and person you was and tried to be for the others that once was an art, tears out your heart.

## My Angel

You are my angel, you are like fragrance of a flower which has just blossomed now.

You are amazing the way you open your heart to all ups and downs of life. You are My Angel.

You are the sweetest person on this earth, some do not see it but soon they will.

You are having ups and downs now, but not to worry just hold your head up your patience and calmness will make it worth it.

You are My Angel.

You are one to feel relaxed to show your joys and sorrows in God and

with God in your Life, your friends will multiply and you can feel better.

You are My Angel.

You are intelligent in ways others are not and that make you uniquely

Special Angel.

## My Friend My Sis

I have a friend who also my sis I found online brought to me by God.

We are far away in miles but we can always make each other smile.

We might not have been born from the moms but we have a bond given to us through God.

We never had to build a friendship it was there day one through God like we blood.

We know when day come we finally meet, be like a seat in heavens gates,

cause it be so great and worth the wait.

## Fire Of My Love

Love I know can increase each day, and for you climbs higher than any forest fire.

If anyone tried to cease the force of my love for you, it would only transpire

into a higher desire to show how much my love increases each day for you, so please do not

be blue since for now I am not with you each each day to see your face and do not think I will be untrue to you.

For the love I have acquires each day as it goes along and passes and sets my

heart spinning, charging through my body to give me chills that wins my soul and takes

control and I know within there is no other that will take my body and soul again.

## Staying Strong

Must stay strong, it feels like too long

since I have praised

you Lord in a song.

I feel I heading back to where I belong.

As you know Lord I been dealing with a lot of woe.

It really hurts deep in my soul

lot of the hurt is very

old buried deep in my soul of my heart.

Just not know how to break it apart

and get it back to my heart

the way it should be.

Must stay Strong,

Help me Lord

to see where you really want my

heart and soul to belong.

## My Little Girl

I look at my little girl face and it so hard to believe
at times
that my baby is a young girl
becoming a young woman before my eyes.

I look at my little girl face and it so hard to believe
that watching her growing up brings tears to my eyes.

I look at my little girl as she smiles
to all the worlds new things for her,
bringing joy to our eyes.

I look at my little girl as she learns
to be seriou
s and all the emotions
of growing up to be a young woman.

I look at my little girl and see in her eyes,
a beautiful, caring, lovely girl
with so much love and more
she will give to all those who come to know
my little girl.

## Shriners Sarge Mom

Sarge Mom always been a fighter
at whatever comes her way,

with a smile and a lot of spunk
to get things done.

Sarge Mom does not let her pain
show she feels at all,

but still has a way of showing
for a while her caring feelings.

Sarge Mom stays tough through it all
as she knows she the one sharing all the time whenever needed.

Sarge Mom knows in the end
the rewards will be worth standing tough.

## Need Me

Just when you need me the most you turn me away, cause you say you in a bad mood, just want you to turn to me, include me, in your bad mood.

I yearn to show you my concern if only you would learn to return my love for you, and stick to me like glue.

As our need for each other flows, and grows as fast as the wind blows when your mood is love, I am included in the woe caused by our hearts that have clicked, so it not matter our love is new, for I sure have the hots for you.

Just know in a bad mood or not I do love you, and want to share the sad with you as much as the glad, to become closer to you as if we together wearing each others shoes, for I am mad about you, in bad mood or not I will always stick with you, and include you, in all I do.

I have been writing poetry since I was 14 I had a lot of poems that accidentally got thrown away when I was younger. I am now 50 years old.
I was born on October 11, 1961

I enjoy writing poetry it is continuously in my thoughts, so many things contribute to how my poems come out in the end.

I am married, have been since February 14, 2000 to a guy I met when I was a sophomore in High School. He was a Freshman. That was in 1977, so we have known each other a long time. He had kids by his first marriage and she basically abandoned them at young ages of 7 years, 5 years, and 13 months. When Robert and I got back together in 1996, kids and I bonded and, well, as time went on I become Mom and I raised his kids with him since 1997 when we all got a home together. I am very glad and proud to their mom and to me they are mine and no one can ever take that away from me or them.

I always felt I had to write my thoughts down so that when I was no longer here I had left something behind, so that others would know the person I really was and the things I encountered in my life. Then they would understand even more of why I made the choices that I did, or the feelings that I felt that I could never explain out loud to anyone.
My Poetry would, but I know now that this is only a small part of my mark that I will leave behind for all who know me and all who do not, because my three kids will be here and their children and so on will know me before I gone and even after when they are all told about me and the person I was and always tried to be for them and others.
So I will be leaving my mark for the world in so many Special ways for Children, Grandchildren, Great Grandchildren, and so on.

I hope all who have and do read my poems enjoy them and can in some way relate to them, and pass the book on to others they know to read and enjoy them as well.

www.ingramcontent.com/pod-product-compliance
Lightning Source LLC
Chambersburg PA
CBHW070942160426
43193CB00011B/1776